A Walk through Our Church

Written and Illustrated by

Gertrud Mueller Nelson

PAULIST PRESS
New York/Mahwah, N.J.

Thanks to Eleanor Bernstein, C.S.J.
Arthur Sikula
Christopher Witt

Jacket design by Saija Autrand, Faces Type and Design

Library of Congress Cataloging-in-Publication Data

Nelson, Gertrud Mueller.
    A walk through our church / by Gertrud Mueller Nelson.
        p.   cm.
    Summary: A brother and sister describe the appearance and significance of various objects they encounter as they walk through an empty church.
    ISBN 0-8091-6648-8 (alk. paper)
    1. Catholic Church buildings—Juvenile literature. 2. Catholic Church—Liturgical objects—Juvenile literature. [1. Catholic Church.] I. Title.
BX1970.3.N45   1998
282—dc21   97-41091
                                                                    CIP
                                                                    AC

Published by Paulist Press
997 Macarthur Boulevard
Mahwah, New Jersey 07430

Printed and bound in Mexico

FOR MY GODCHILDREN:

Joseph David
Anne Loretta
Christian
Simon Joseph
Catherine Elizabeth
Deana Kay
Michael Joseph
John Benjamin
Michael David
Nannie Sinclair
Marky
Janet-Marie
Andrew Thomas
Margaret Valerie
Miguel Hun+

A Walk through Our Church

My mom takes us to church. She has a meeting in the school hall. She wants my brother and me to wait for her.

I tell my brother: "Let's go up the steps
and go in the church.
Let's look at everything
and you tell me about what we see!"

"Ok," says my brother. "Let's."

I'll ask my brother lots of questions.

Let us go rejoicing to the house of our God.

3

We step in the door and what do we see?
The first thing we see is a pool of clear water.
My brother shows me how we bless ourselves with this
water.

"Why do we do that? Why do we bless ourselves?"
    "So we remember the day of our baptism."
"This is where I was baptized, right?"
    "Right! So was I."
"Why did we get baptized?"
    "Baptism means we become members of God's
    family and share in the life of Jesus."

Because we are baptized, God's house is our house too.

The pool is called the *baptismal font.*
We bless ourselves with *holy water.*

We dip our fingers into this water,
make a cross over ourselves and say:

**In the name of the Father, and of the Son and
of the Holy Spirit.**

By the pool stands the biggest candle I have ever seen!
I remember how we light this candle for the first time in
the holy night of Easter.

My brother says: "It stands here to remind us of
Jesus, the light of the world, who lives among us and
is always with us."
"Do we light it for other days?"
"We light this candle for every baptism and
every funeral that happens through the year."

This is to show that one day, like Jesus,
we will live forever.

The big candle is called the *Easter candle* or the *Paschal candle.*

Light of Christ! Thanks be to God!

Over on the wall I see a little cupboard with a glass door. We can see inside. On a shelf are three tall bottles.

I ask my brother what the bottles are for.
    "In each bottle there is holy oil," he tells me.

    "One bottle has the oil of the sick.
      The priest uses that one to bless sick people.
      It comforts them. It heals their sadness.
      It forgives their sins."

This blessing is a *sacrament.*
It is called the *sacrament of the sick.*
The oil is called the *oil of the sick.*
The little cupboard where the oils are kept
is called the *ambry.*

This is my comfort in my trouble, that your promise gives me life.

9

"In the second bottle is oil given to people who are getting ready for baptism. They are blessed with it to make them strong while they learn what it means to be baptized and to keep the promises made at baptism."

People getting ready for baptism are called *catechumens*. This oil is called *the oil of catechumens*.

Will you strive for justice and peace among all people and respect every human being? I will.

"The third bottle has oil in it too. It is made from squeezed olives, just like the other oils, but this one has a beautiful smell. The good smell comes from crushed flowers and herbs which are mixed in. This is the oil used in baptism, confirmation and holy orders. A person receives a blessing on the forehead with this oil. Kings were blessed with oil when they were crowned. Priests are anointed with oil when they are made priests. We are all anointed when we are baptized and confirmed."

We are all made part of God's royal priesthood.

This oil is called *holy chrism*.

May those who are sealed with this oil of chrism share in the royal priesthood of Jesus Christ.

10

Here in a quiet corner of our church is a little chapel. It has two chairs and a kneeler. You can meet the priest here for the sacrament of forgiveness. You can sit here and talk with the priest when you have sinned.

Sometimes we decide to be mean or selfish or lazy.

Sometimes we disobey or tell lies or are greedy, even when we know better!

The priest talks to us about how we can set things right. Then we kneel at the kneeler. We tell Jesus we are sorry. We promise to do better.

Jesus takes away our sins.

This room is called the *chapel of reconciliation.*

Show me your way, O Lord.
Lead me on a level path.

Now we leave the back of the church and walk down the aisle. We look all around. This church is a big place. The ceiling is high. There are big windows of colored glass. A few have pictures of Jesus and the saints.

My brother shows me his favorite window.
It is a picture of some saints.

"I guess saints are people the light shines through!"

I have my favorite window too. I even know the story in that window myself. It is a picture of Jesus, the Good Shepherd.

The sun shines through the glass and sends patches of color on us and all around us.

The colored glass is called *stained glass.*

Look upon God and be radiant.

15

We sit down in one of the benches.
There is a book here for each person.
The book has songs to help us sing all together when we
gather for a celebration.

"Why do we sing in church?"

"When we sing these songs,
  we are singing our prayers.
  Maybe singing makes our praise twice as strong!"

Some churches use chairs.
The benches are called *pews*.
The songs we sing in church are called *hymns*
and the song book is called a *hymnal*.

**My tongue will shout your goodness,
and sing your praises all day long.**

17

All the pews are arranged to face the front.
They face a special place.

"What do we call this place?"

"It is called the *sanctuary.*
Sanctuary means 'holy place.'"

In the sanctuary I see a big cross, a large table, a reading stand and a special chair. The cross hangs high—like a blessing—over this holy place. To one side is the reading stand. In another place is the special chair.

Holy, holy, holy. Lord God of hosts.

GMN

19

I look at the large cross with a figure of Jesus on it. Jesus died on the cross and then after three days he became alive again. Now he lives forever. On this cross, Jesus looks strong and brave.

"Why does Jesus look brave?"

> "Because he wants us to remember that dying is hard but then, after we die, don't forget, he will gather us up in his open arms."

Jesus will take us to live with him forever.

On Good Friday, when we especially remember Jesus on the cross, a cross is placed on a cushion. We all go up to kneel before the cross and think about this. Some people kiss the cross. Some people touch the cross. Some people bow very low.

A cross with an image of Jesus is called a *crucifix*.

Christ has died.
Christ is risen.
Christ will come again.

I know about this big chair.
This chair is where the priest sits when someone else reads to us.

> "The priest sits there quietly while we all think about God's story."

Because the priest leads us in prayer when we gather, the priest is called the *one who presides*.
So the chair is called the *president's chair*.

We have waited in silence on your loving-kindness, O God, in the midst of your temple.

If we are quiet, we may come into the sanctuary. I promise my brother that I will walk with quiet feet. I stand at the book stand and look out into the church. Now I know what it feels like to read the word of the Lord.

Some Sundays our mom reads at this book stand. This book she reads from has a special reading for every celebration.
    "The first reading mostly tells about the Hebrew people and God's love for them.
    The second reading is often a letter written by one of the first Christians."

After the first two readings, everybody stands up tall and sings *Alleluia!* That means it is time for the priest to read us the Gospel story from this book. It is a holy story.

"Is that why the book has this beautiful cover?"
    "Yes. And that's why people hold the book high and bow before it. The priest even kisses the page because Jesus speaks to us through holy words."

When we hear the stories from this book, we meet Jesus in a special way. Then the priest preaches about those stories.

The book stand is called the *pulpit* or the *ambo*.
The book with God's word is called *the lectionary.*
Alleluia means "Praise to God."
Gospel means "good news."
When the priest preaches, we call that the *homily.*

The word of the Lord. Thanks be to God.

At Sunday celebrations, many people fill the church.
We listen to the words. "Why else do we come here
every Sunday?"

> My brother tells me: "We gather around this table to
> remember God's gift to us: God's son, Jesus.
> We remember the meal Jesus shared with his
> friends. We give thanks to God. We offer our gifts
> and our selves with Jesus to God."

At the big table the priest prepares a holy meal for us.
The priest prays the great prayer of thanksgiving.
When we pray this prayer and remember what Jesus
did, then Jesus is with us in a special way.
Bread and wine become our holy food.

> When we eat this holy food, we take Jesus into our
> hearts. We are the body of Christ.

That's a sign of how much Jesus loves us and wants us
to be together.

The table of the Lord is called the *altar.*
The holy meal is called the *eucharist*
Eucharist means *thanksgiving.*

O taste and see the goodness of the Lord.

Around the altar are candles. Servers get to light these candles before a celebration begins.
My brother and his friends are servers.

> My brother says: "Candles pray with us as they burn."

> Candles also say: "This place and what happens here is important."

Just like we light candles at home for special dinners! This is God's special dinner.

One day I plan to be a server and light those candles too!

Those who help in the celebration are called *servers*.

Praise God in this holy temple!

Now we come to a quiet place. I like it here. Light pours down from a window overhead. It shines on a beautiful, jeweled box.

I know what is in this box. In the box the priest keeps some of the eucharistic bread left over from our celebration.

> It is kept for the people who are too sick or too old to come to church. Someone will bring the bread to them in their homes or in the hospital. This way they can be one with Jesus and one with this whole family of Jesus.

We all share the same feast, and the sick and the old people won't be left out.

This place is called the *place of reservation.*
The box is called the *tabernacle.*

Give us this day our daily bread.

I know that the eucharistic bread is here in this tabernacle because a lamp hangs here, glowing. When that lamp is burning, it means: Jesus is here in the eucharist. Pay attention.

The lamp that tells us Jesus is here in the holy bread is called the *sanctuary lamp.*

You, O Lord, are my light and my salvation.

33

Near the sanctuary is a place where singers stand on Sundays. They stand by the *organ.* The organ is like a piano that you play with your hands and your feet at the same time. Our organ has many pipes.

They look like giant whistles and the music just blows right out of them!

Sometimes those pipes sound like flutes and sometimes they sound like thunder!

An organ can make powerful music.

Sometimes we use other instruments too: a piano, a guitar, a violin or a flute.

The person who leads our singing is called the *cantor.* The group who helps us sing is called the *choir.*

Sing to the Lord a new song for God has done wonderful deeds.

The central celebrations in our church are baptism and the eucharistic meal. But there are some other ways to pray in church.

Here is a way we like to pray, especially during the season of Lent, when we prepare our hearts for Easter: All around the wall are fifteen pictures. The pictures tell the story of how Jesus carried the cross, suffered, died, was buried and rose up from death again. You can walk slowly from picture to picture and think about what you see there. Then you say a prayer at each picture.

These pictures are called *stations of the cross.*

We adore you, O Christ, and we bless you, because by your holy cross you have redeemed the world.

My brother takes me into a room full of cupboards, clos-
ets and drawers. My brother knows this room because
he is a server. All the important things for our worship
are kept here when they are not in use. It is the room
where the servers put on their special robes and where
the priest puts on special clothes as well.

> When the priest and the servers put on these robes
> it tells us that the gathering about to happen is no
> ordinary gathering.

We all wear our good clothes when we come to church
on Sundays.
It helps us remember that this is no ordinary day.

This room is called the *sacristy.*

**I will serve you faithfully all the days of my
life.**

A large closet holds the priest's special clothes. This is what a priest wears for the celebration of eucharist:

A long white linen robe, called an *alb*. The word *alb* means "white."

Then a big, colored garment with a hole in the middle for the head. This garment covers the priest almost completely. This garment is called the *chasuble*.

Over the shoulders, the priest wears a long, beautiful strip of cloth. This strip of cloth is called a *stole*.

All these special clothes are called *vestments*.

Each feast and season has its own color of chasuble and stole:
white for the feasts of Jesus and Mary;
red for the feasts of the Holy Spirit and those saints who gave their lives for Jesus, the martyrs;
midnight purple for Advent, when we get ready for Christmas;
purple for Lent, when we get ready for Easter;
green for all the Sundays in between, called *ordinary time*.

May this priest exalt you, O Lord, in the midst of your people.

Over here, I notice the offering baskets. These baskets are passed during the celebration on Sundays. As the baskets are passed from hand to hand, people drop in some money.

It's a small sign of themselves and of the work they do all week.
It makes everyday work become part of God's work.

Sometimes I bring some of my allowance and drop it in the basket.

Some of this money is used to help the poor.

The coins I drop in the basket are called an *offering*.

Accept, O Lord, the work of my hands to the glory of your kingdom.

My brother shows me a brass dish with a lid full of holes. It hangs on a chain. It is used on special feasts. This dish will be filled with good-smelling spices and tree sap from faraway lands. When this is burned, thick, sweet-smelling smoke comes pouring through the holes in the lid. It fills the air. The servers and then the priest pour this smoke over everything that deserves this blessing: the altar, the lectionary, the priest.

They swing it over all of us to honor us too! Then they bow and we bow back. I really like that part.

Incense is valuable and precious, my brother tells me. When we praise God, I guess we just want to waste the very best we have!

The holy smoke is called *incense.*
The kings brought Jesus incense at Bethlehem.
The brass bowl from which the smoke pours
is called the *censer* or a *thurible.*
The server who carries the *censer* or *thurible* is called the *thurifer.*

Like burning incense may my prayer rise up to you, O Lord.

In a special cabinet they keep the holiest cup and plate when they don't need them at the altar.

> This is the cup which holds the wine that becomes the blood of Christ, the cup of salvation.
> The plate will hold the bread which becomes the body of Christ, the bread of heaven.

The holy cup is called the *chalice.*
The special plate is sometimes called a *paten.*
The bread is called the *host* or *eucharistic bread.*

I will lift the cup of salvation and call upon the name of the Lord.

On a stand is a beautiful cross on a long pole. This is the cross that leads the parade into church on Sunday morning. Servers follow it. Another comes swinging the censer with the incense. Then the reader comes holding the book up high. Last comes the priest to begin the celebration.

But the cross comes first. Everybody in the church is singing.

In church, a parade is called a *procession*.
The cross on the pole is called the *processional cross*.

Let the assembly of the peoples gather round you.

49

Over in that peaceful corner there is a wooden image of Mary. She is standing on the moon. She shines like the sun. Around her head are twelve stars. Mary is the mother of Jesus. She is our heavenly mother too.

All around her are little candles. On quiet days when the church is almost empty, people kneel here and talk to Mary. They tell Mary their needs and give her their thanks. Sometimes, since they can't stay and pray all day, they light a candle and let the candle keep on praying for them until it finally burns out.

Today, there are many candles burning. My eyes want to watch the flames flicker and wave. Up and down. Up and down. That means there is a lot of praying going on around here! Everybody's praying together.

The image of Mary is called a *statue.*
The candles are called *votive lights.*

Hail, Mary, full of grace.
The Lord is with thee.

51

Over by the side door is a little box built into the wall. It says: "For the Poor." It has a slot to drop in coins. The coins are used to buy food and medicines for the poor.

When something goes especially well for me and I am happy, I like to say an extra *thank you:* I put a coin into that box so that my happiness spreads all around to others.

This box is called the *poor box.*
The money we give to the needy is called *alms.*

Happy are they who consider the poor and needy!
The Lord will deliver them in the time of trouble.

We walked a big circle all around the church. Now it's time to pray quietly. My brother and I go back to the altar of reservation.

We bow down on one knee and greet Jesus present there in the holy bread.
This bow is called a *genuflection*.
Then we bow our heads.

When we stand up again, we each go to a kneeler to pray.

> It is very quiet here.
> I let the quiet wash over me.
> It hushes the noise in my busy brain.
> I let myself go into the silence.
> When I am still, I just breathe.
> I breathe God in. Then I breathe God out.
> In and out. In and out.
> In stillness I wait to hear what God wants me to hear.

Be still before the Lord and wait patiently.

Now it is time to go home. Our mom will be waiting for us outside. But I know something: on Sunday morning our whole family will come back. So will everybody else. We will all meet and greet each other here. We will all go up the steps into the church and through the wide doors for the eucharistic celebration.

In and out. In and out. The church breathes us....
It breathes us in and it breathes us out.

Right now, we are going out.

I go out to love and serve the Lord.